YOUR
DIGESTIVE SYSTEM

Understand It with Numbers

Melanie Waldron

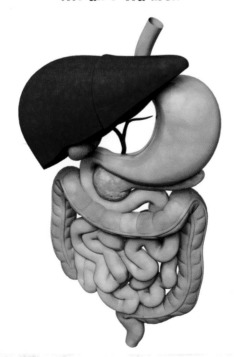

Chicago, Illinois

Produced for Raintree by
White-Thomson Publishing
www.wtpub.co.uk
+44 (0)843 208 7460

Edited by Rachel Minay
Designed by Basement68
Original illustrations © Capstone 2014
Illustrated by HL Studios
Picture research by Rachel Minay/
Melanie Waldron
Production by Victoria Fitzgerald
Originated by Capstone Global Library Ltd
Printed and bound in China by CTPS

17 16 15 14 13
10 9 8 7 6 5 4 3 2 1

**Library of Congress Cataloging-in-Publication
Data**
Waldron, Melanie.
  Your digestive system : understand it with
numbers / Melanie Waldron.
    pages cm.—(Your body by numbers)
  Includes bibliographical references and index.
  ISBN 978-1-4109-5982-9 (hb)—ISBN 978-
1-4109-5987-4 (pb) 1. Digestion—Juvenile
literature. 2. Digestive organs—Juvenile
literature. I. Title.

QP145.W23 2014
612.3—dc23   2013016817

Acknowledgments
The author and publisher are grateful to
the following for permission to reproduce
copyright material:
Corbis pp. 5 (© Randy Faris), 12 (© Barry Lewis/
In Pictures), 27 (© Photo Quest Ltd/Science
Photo Library), 41 (© David Turnley); Getty
pp. 9 (Cultura Science/Joseph Giacomin), 17
bottom (AFP/Getty Images), 29 (Jupiterimages),
43 (Sean Justice), HL Studios pp. 8, 11 top,
16, 18, 23 top, 24, 26, 28, 31 top, 34, 36 top,
40; Shutterstock pp. front cover and i (dream
designs), 3 (Valeriy Lebedev), 4 (spotmatik), 7
top (Wutthichai), 7 bottom (Rachel Brunette),
9 inset a (Valentina Razumova), 9 inset b (Olga
Miltsova), 9 inset c (M. Unal Ozmen), 9 inset d
(Andrey Shtanko), 10 (CLS Design), 11 bottom
(Johan Swanepoel), 13 top (Nathalie Speliers
Ufermann), 13 bottom (Valeriy Lebedev), 14 top
(Yusuf YILMAZ), 14 bottom (Greg Amptman),
15 top (kurhan), 15 bottom (Lusoimages), 17
top (Africa Studio), 19 top (Popov Nikolay),
19 bottom (CREATISTA), 20 (Blaj Gabriel),
21 (Monkey Business Images), 22 (Dmitry
Lobanov), 23 bottom (saurabhpbhoyar), 25
(CLIPAREA/Custom media), 28–29 (Monkik),
30 (2xSamara.com), 31 bottom (Valentyn
Volkov), 33 left (Anna Kucherova), 33 right
(Madlen), 35 (Dmitry Naumov), 36 (Villiers
Steyn), 37 top (O2creationz), 37 bottom
(Joevoz), 38a (saiko3p), 38b (Ensuper), 38c
(Ian 2010), 38d (MidoSemsem), 38e (Pavlo
Loushkin), 38f (Picsfive), 39 (ruigsantos), 42
(GRei), 44 (Pavlo Loushkin), 47 (Lusoimages);
SuperStock pp. 6 (DR LR/BSIP), 32 (age
footstock).

Every effort has been made to contact copyright
holders of any material reproduced in this book.
Any omissions will be rectified in subsequent
printings if notice is given to the publisher.

CONTENTS

Some words are shown in bold,
like this. You can find out what they
mean by looking in the glossary.

A Food Factory

So, what is your digestive system? It's like a factory that your body uses to process all the food and drink you consume. It is really a long tube going all through your body from your mouth to your anus (the opening at your bottom). Various things happen at different stages along the digestive system. Its main purpose is to extract from your food and drink all the things your body needs to keep you healthy.

Eating is good! Not only does food taste yummy, it also keeps your body healthy. Your digestive system gets to work on everything you eat and drink.

A Long Journey?

Food travels down from your mouth and through your digestive system. Parts of what you eat will come out the other end, as feces (poop). The time it takes to go from mouth to toilet depends on the type of food eaten. It is also different for different people. So there is no "normal" length of time. But for most people, the time taken will be anywhere between 12 and 72 hours.

Many Meals

Say you eat three meals a day, seven days a week, 52 weeks a year, for 75 years—that's 3 x 7 x 52 x 75 = 81,900 meals in a lifetime! Your digestive system has to process all these meals. It's not just your mouth and stomach that do the work. There are other parts of the digestive system, including your **intestines**. Your body has other parts that get rid of liquid waste in the form of urine (pee). So what are these body parts, and what do they all do?

How often does your family make a big supermarket trip? Does it surprise you how quickly you get through all that food and drink?

Food, Glorious Food

We all know that (most) food is yummy to eat, but what else does it do? Different foods contain different amounts of chemicals that your body needs.

Vitamins

Lots of different foods contain vitamins. There are 13 different vitamins, such as vitamin A (retinol) and vitamin C (ascorbic acid). Your body needs vitamins to help it do lots of different jobs, such as keeping bones and blood healthy and fighting disease and infection.

Rickets

Rickets is a condition that can be caused by a lack of vitamin D. This vitamin helps the body to control levels of minerals such as calcium and phosphate. If there is not enough vitamin D, the body can start to release calcium and phosphate from the bones. This makes them weak and soft, and they can start to bend. Vitamin D, however, is not just provided by food—in fact, you only get about 10 percent of your daily requirement through food. The rest is provided by sunlight! Your skin makes this vitamin when sunlight falls on it.

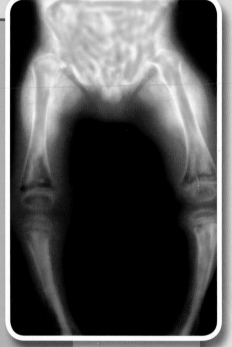

This X-ray shows how rickets has caused the legs to bend outward at the knee.

Minerals

Many foods contain **minerals**. Your body needs over 20 different minerals, including calcium, magnesium, phosphorous, potassium, and sodium. Minerals help your body to build new **tissues**. They help your muscles to work, and your blood to **clot** if you cut yourself. They also help your body to extract the energy contained in your food.

Some people take vitamin and mineral pills. But for most people, eating a healthy, balanced diet with plenty of fruits and vegetables will mean they get all the vitamins and minerals they need.

Energy-Givers

Your body needs energy. It gets energy from chemicals in food called carbohydrates. There are several types of carbohydrates, which include sugars and starches. We can't digest some carbohydrates, and we call these fiber. There are lots of different sugars in food—not just the stuff you buy in packets. Pasta, bread, rice, and potatoes are all high in carbohydrates.

You also get energy from fats in your food. Fats have another important job—they bind to vitamins and help to carry them around in your blood. Foods high in fats include butter, cheese, oils, and oily fish.

You get some energy from **proteins** in your food. Proteins are also needed for building and repairing muscles and bones. Meat, fish, and eggs contain a lot of protein, and so do nuts, seeds, and **pulses** such as lentils.

The flames in this diagram represent energy. The diagram shows that fats give more than twice the amount of energy, gram for gram, than protein or carbohydrates. This is why it is important not to have too much fat in your diet—consuming more energy than your body uses will cause it to store this as fat.

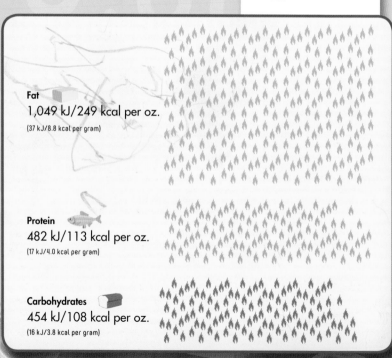

Fat
1,049 kJ/249 kcal per oz.
(37 kJ/8.8 kcal per gram)

Protein
482 kJ/113 kcal per oz.
(17 kJ/4.0 kcal per gram)

Carbohydrates
454 kJ/108 kcal per oz.
(16 kJ/3.8 kcal per gram)

Burning It Up

Your body's digestive system extracts all the energy that your body needs to stay alive. You need energy for warmth, and for keeping **organs** such as your heart and brain working. You also need energy to make all of your movements. The more you move, the more energy you need.

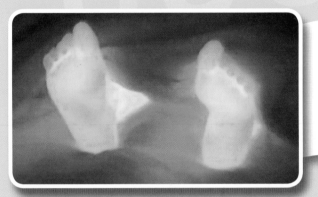

Even when you might think you are doing nothing, your body is busy. It needs energy to keep you warm and alive. This thermal image shows that even a person at rest is giving off heat energy.

Food	Feet (Meters)
Apple	1,600 (500)
Egg	3,300 (1,000)
Slice of bread	4,000 (1,200)
Portion of chicken	5,000 (1,500)
Two scoops of ice cream	8,200 (2,500)
Bar of chocolate	11,500 (3,500)
Package of peanuts	14,100 (4,300)

This table gives rough estimates of the distances you could run on the energy supplied by different foods.

9

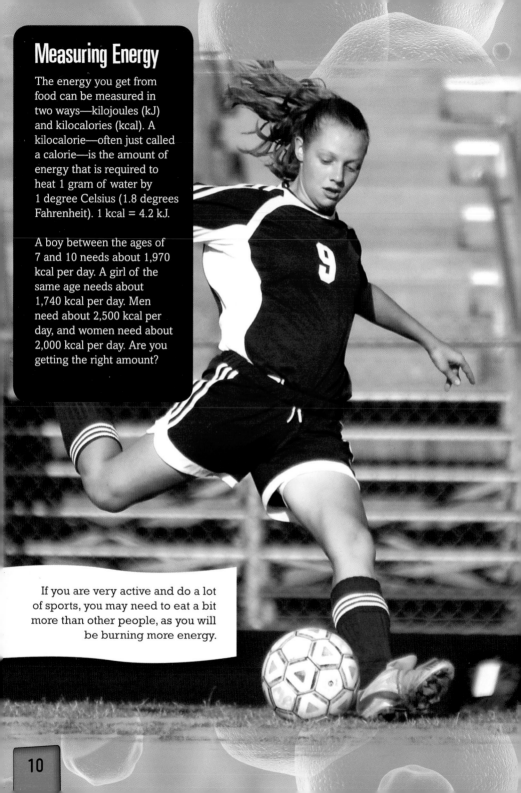

Measuring Energy

The energy you get from food can be measured in two ways—kilojoules (kJ) and kilocalories (kcal). A kilocalorie—often just called a calorie—is the amount of energy that is required to heat 1 gram of water by 1 degree Celsius (1.8 degrees Fahrenheit). 1 kcal = 4.2 kJ.

A boy between the ages of 7 and 10 needs about 1,970 kcal per day. A girl of the same age needs about 1,740 kcal per day. Men need about 2,500 kcal per day, and women need about 2,000 kcal per day. Are you getting the right amount?

If you are very active and do a lot of sports, you may need to eat a bit more than other people, as you will be burning more energy.

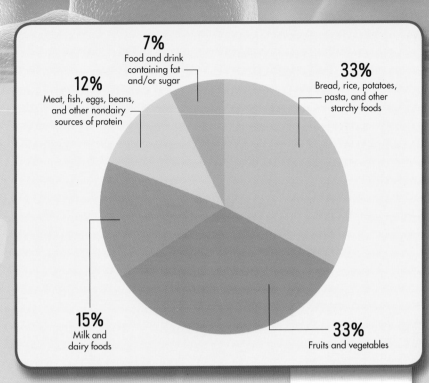

7%
Food and drink containing fat and/or sugar

33%
Bread, rice, potatoes, pasta, and other starchy foods

12%
Meat, fish, eggs, beans, and other nondairy sources of protein

15%
Milk and dairy foods

33%
Fruits and vegetables

Food Mountains

Over your lifetime, you will drink around 20,000 gallons (75,000 liters) of liquid and eat around 50 tons of food. This is around the weight of six elephants! Around two-thirds of all that food is used by your body to give you energy for heat, growth, and movement, and to repair your tissues. So make sure you eat well!

This pie chart shows the percentages of different food types that make up a healthy diet.

Elephant Appetites!

How much food do you think you eat in a day? Elephants chomp through 328–373 pounds (149–169 kilograms) every day! That's about the weight of two average men. Elephants spend about 80 percent of their day nibbling away at grasses, small plants, bushes, fruit, twigs, tree bark, and roots.

Open Wide!

The first part of your digestive system is, of course, your mouth! So what goes on there?

Making Your Mouth Water

Your digestive system starts getting to work even before you put food in your mouth. You usually smell it first, using smell-sensing **nerve cells** in your nose. There are 10 million of these tiny little sensors there! When you are hungry, the smell of food makes your mouth start producing more saliva.

Saliva is a clear liquid that comes from six little organs in your mouth called salivary **glands**. Saliva is around 99 percent water. The other 1 percent is made up of chemicals including **enzymes**. One of these enzymes is called amylase. Amylase gets to work on the starch in your food and starts breaking it down.

Animals make saliva, too—some more than others!

Making Saliva

Your mouth makes over 2 pints (1 liter) of saliva every day! In two months, you will make over 127 pints (60 liters)—enough to take a bath in! If you live for 75 years, you will have made over 57,000 pints (27,000 liters) of saliva in your lifetime.

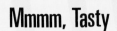

Mmmm, Tasty

Your tongue is covered in around 10,000 taste buds. These are tiny little bumps with nerve cells that detect different flavors in food. Your tongue also pushes and moves food around your mouth. This means you get the full effect of the food passing over all your taste buds! It also means you can mush up the food.

Terrific Tongues

How big do you think your tongue is—about the size of a crushed pear? Compare this to the tongue of the giant blue whale—it weighs as much as an elephant!

13

Chomping Your Food

Your jaws get to work on the food in your mouth. They clamp down on the food, and your teeth slice and grind the food up into smaller pieces. In your lifetime, you have two sets of teeth. Babies usually get their first teeth at around the age of six months. Young children have 20 teeth. From about the age of six, these baby teeth start to drop out, and adult teeth start to grow in their place. Most adults have 32 teeth. Can you count your teeth?

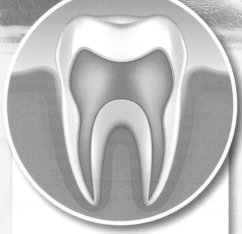

The part of a tooth that you can see makes up about one-third of the total length of the tooth. Two-thirds of the tooth are below the gum. Gums hold the teeth in place.

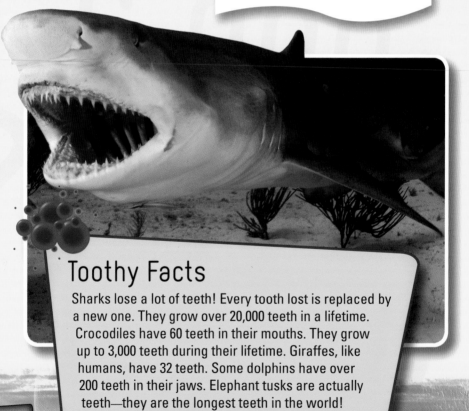

Toothy Facts

Sharks lose a lot of teeth! Every tooth lost is replaced by a new one. They grow over 20,000 teeth in a lifetime. Crocodiles have 60 teeth in their mouths. They grow up to 3,000 teeth during their lifetime. Giraffes, like humans, have 32 teeth. Some dolphins have over 200 teeth in their jaws. Elephant tusks are actually teeth—they are the longest teeth in the world!

Harder Than Nails

The hard, shiny outer coat of your teeth is called enamel. It is the hardest substance in your body. But enamel is not indestructible. It can be attacked by **bacteria** in plaque. Plaque is a substance that forms on teeth after eating food—particularly sugary food. Plaque needs to be brushed away to stop your teeth from decaying (rotting).

Wisdom Teeth

Many adults don't have a full set of 32 teeth. The last four to grow, called wisdom teeth, usually appear between the ages of 17 and 25.

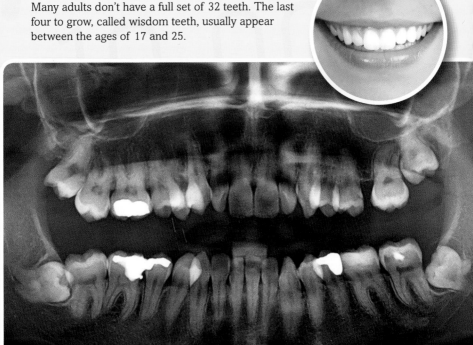

You can see this person's wisdom teeth still in the gums, and a gap where a tooth has been lost. The bright white areas are fillings in the teeth.

Making Mush

Your food is sliced and crushed by your teeth. Your tongue mixes in saliva to create mushy blobs of food that are easy to swallow. You can exert quite a bit of pressure using your jaw muscles when you chew!

Pressure can be measured in units called psi, which stands for pounds of weight per square inch. Your jaws can create a psi of 120. Compare this to the pressure inside your bicycle tire when you pump it up—this is only around 40 psi.

This bar chart shows the bite pressure of humans compared to some animals. A crocodile has an enormous bite pressure—best to keep away!

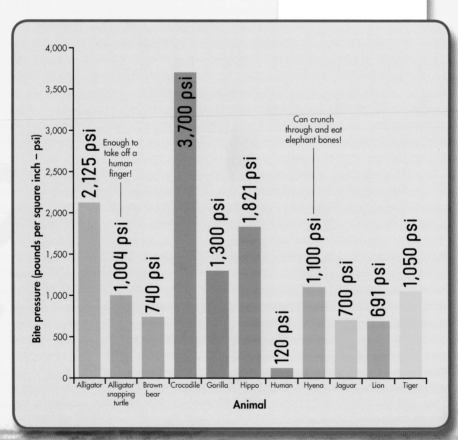

Bite pressure (pounds per square inch – psi) vs. Animal

- Alligator: 2,125 psi
- Alligator snapping turtle: 1,004 psi — Enough to take off a human finger!
- Brown bear: 740 psi
- Crocodile: 3,700 psi
- Gorilla: 1,300 psi
- Hippo: 1,821 psi
- Human: 120 psi
- Hyena: 1,100 psi — Can crunch through and eat elephant bones!
- Jaguar: 700 psi
- Lion: 691 psi
- Tiger: 1,050 psi

Gulp!

The mushy blobs of food in your mouth start getting digested (broken down) in your mouth by the enzymes in your saliva. The enzymes break down starches, and they become sugars. Try chewing some bread, which is a starchy food. After a while, do you notice that it starts to taste a bit sweeter?

When you are ready to swallow, your tongue pushes the mush to the back of your throat. Your windpipe, which goes down into your lungs, closes off so that the food doesn't go down there and choke you. Instead, the food enters another pipe, called the gullet or esophagus. This is about 10 inches (25 centimeters) long and about 1 inch (2 centimeters) thick.

Some people train for years to learn how to "swallow" swords. They manage to override their body's swallow reflex. It is extremely dangerous!

Autopilot

Swallowing is an automatic **reflex**. This means that you can't control it or stop it once it has started. It starts when your tongue pushes the food to the back of your throat.

The Stomach Churner

At the bottom end of your esophagus, your food squeezes through a narrow gap and into a j-shaped bag. This is your stomach, and the next stage of digestion happens here.

Incredible Expansion

Your stomach sits at the bottom of your esophagus, on the left side of your body. It sits just under the bottom part of your ribcage. When your stomach is empty, it is about the size of your fist, up to 0.16 pint (75 milliliters). But the stomach is an amazingly stretchy organ. It can expand to over 4.2 pints (2 liters) during a big meal with drinks!

Empty stomach
**0.16 pint
(75 ml)**

Very full stomach
**4.2 pints
(2,000 ml)**

Milk

WHOLE MILK

The volume of a stomach can expand up to 27 times its empty volume—after a very large meal!

Acid Attack

Your stomach contains different liquids that are important for digestion. These liquids are called gastric juices. They include a chemical called hydrochloric acid and enzymes. All these chemicals start the process of breaking down your food into smaller and smaller chemical parts called molecules. Further down your digestive system, your body can absorb (take in) these small molecules. The acid in the gastric juices usually kills any germs that get into your stomach.

The gastric juices are released from 3 million little holes in the wall of your stomach called gastric pits. The chemicals are so strong that without protection they would begin to dissolve the wall of your stomach. But your stomach wall also releases **mucus**. This coats the stomach wall and stops the gastric juices from dissolving it.

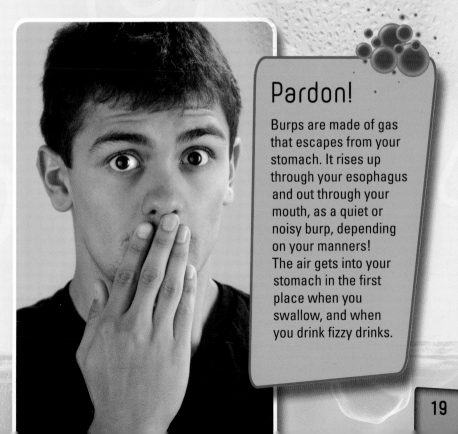

Pardon!

Burps are made of gas that escapes from your stomach. It rises up through your esophagus and out through your mouth, as a quiet or noisy burp, depending on your manners! The air gets into your stomach in the first place when you swallow, and when you drink fizzy drinks.

Coming Back Up!

Eeurghh! Vomiting happens when your stomach squeezes tightly and pushes its contents back up and out through your mouth. It is caused by lots of things, including eating rotten food, eating too much food, feeling dizzy, being nervous, or being unwell. If your stomach squeezes violently, it can project the vomit up to nearly 10 feet (3 meters)!

Vomit tastes of the strong gastric juices from the stomach and makes a burning feeling in the mouth and nose. The stomach acid in the gastric juices can rot teeth if someone vomits a lot. The body tries to defend the teeth from this acid attack by producing lots of saliva just before vomiting.

Usually your body gives you some warning that you are about to throw up.

How Often Do You Vomit?

No one likes vomiting, so it's a good thing that it doesn't happen often. Pity whales, though—they vomit around once a week! They do this to get rid of things they can't digest.

Muscle–Churning

The muscles in your stomach wall contract and expand around every 20 seconds. This churns the food inside and mixes it with the gastric juices. After about three to four hours, your stomach starts to send squirts of this churned-up food through an opening at the bottom of your stomach. Here the food passes into your intestines.

Brainy Stomachs?

Did you know there are around 500 million nerve cells in your digestive system? They send and receive signals from your brain. The signals tell your brain how hungry or full you are. When you feel hungry, your brain is telling you that you need to eat. But when you start eating, it takes about 20 minutes for the message to get to your brain to tell you that you are not hungry anymore!

Eat slowly, to give your brain time to catch up with signals coming from your digestive system!

Digestive Organs

There are some organs in your body, near your stomach, that help your digestive system to work properly. These are your pancreas, liver, and gallbladder.

Juicy Pancreas

The pancreas is a long, pink, soft, and floppy organ that lies just behind your stomach. It makes gastric juices—around 3.2 pints (1.5 liters) a day. These juices contain lots of different enzymes. They all help to break down different parts of food—for example, proteins, starches, and fats. The juices pass along a small tube called the pancreatic duct and into your intestines, just below your stomach.

Your pancreas is about the size of your hand. Around 90 percent of it makes the enzymes, and the other 10 percent makes chemicals called **insulin** and **glucagon**. These chemicals control the level of sugar in your blood.

Diabetes

Some people have a condition called type 1 diabetes. This is when the pancreas cannot make insulin. Their blood sugar levels can become too high or too low. They may have to inject themselves with insulin to control the blood sugar levels.

This bar chart shows safe blood sugar levels for a person without diabetes and a person with type 1 diabetes. One measurement is for just before a meal, and the other is for two hours after a meal, when blood sugar levels rise.

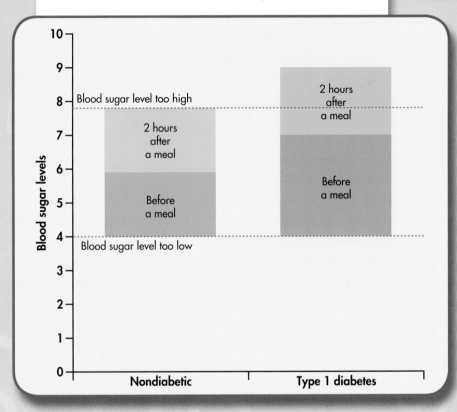

Diabetes and Diet

Around 85–95 percent of **diabetic** adults have a kind of diabetes called type 2 diabetes. This is when the pancreas does not make enough insulin, or the insulin it makes doesn't work properly. People with type 2 diabetes can control their blood sugar levels by carefully monitoring the amount of sugar in their diet.

Lumpy Liver

The second biggest organ in your body, after your skin, is your liver. A liver weighs about 3.3 pounds (1.5 kilograms) and sits just behind your lower-right ribs. The liver is made of thousands of tiny six-sided lumps the size of a pinhead. It is dark red because of all the blood in it.

Your liver does more than 500 different processes in your body! It gets going on all the chemicals and nutrients in your blood after a big meal. As it does this, it produces about 20 percent of your body's warmth.

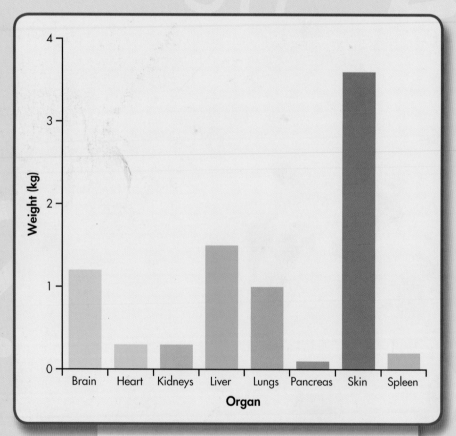

There are almost 80 different organs in your body. This bar chart shows the weights of the eight heaviest. The liver and the pancreas are both in the top eight.

Helping Digestion

One of the jobs of your liver is to make a substance called bile. This is used to break down fats in your food. Bile also contains things that the body wants to get rid of, such as bilirubin, a yellowish liquid that your body makes when it is getting rid of dead red blood cells. Bile is stored underneath your liver in a pouch called the gallbladder. It passes from this into your intestines.

This picture shows the position of the liver in the body.

Nutrient Factory

Blood travels from your intestines and into your liver. Here, nutrients in the blood get broken down into smaller molecules that your body can use. Your liver can store some vitamins and minerals for your body to use when it needs them. It also breaks down harmful substances in the blood, such as alcohol.

Regrowing Liver

Livers can regrow if they get damaged. You can lose up to 90 percent of your liver—and still survive! Your liver will grow new material to become the right size again.

In the Intestines

When it is ready, the food churned up by your stomach enters your intestines. Here, nutrients are extracted from the food for your body to use. There are two parts to the intestines—the small intestines and the large intestines.

Small (but Long) Intestines

The first part of the small intestines is called the duodenum. Food mixes with bile (from the gallbladder) and pancreatic juices (from the pancreas). Now your body can begin to extract nutrients.

The small intestines are about 21 feet (6.5 meters) long but only 0.8 inch (2 centimeters) wide—this is why they are called small. They lie all curled up inside your **abdomen**. They are this length so that there is enough time to break down all the food as it passes through and extract the nutrients the body needs. The food travels through at about 1 inch (2.5 centimeters) per minute. The small intestines also make some gastric juices to help with digestion.

This diagram shows the amount of digestive juices made at different places in the digestive system. Your small intestines make the most!

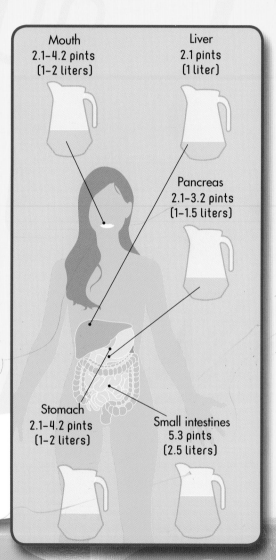

Mouth
2.1–4.2 pints
(1–2 liters)

Liver
2.1 pints
(1 liter)

Pancreas
2.1–3.2 pints
(1–1.5 liters)

Stomach
2.1–4.2 pints
(1–2 liters)

Small intestines
5.3 pints
(2.5 liters)

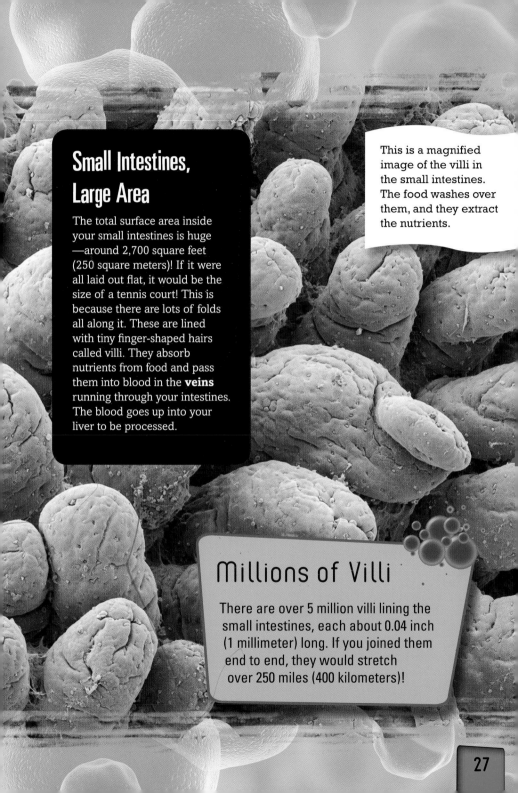

Small Intestines, Large Area

The total surface area inside your small intestines is huge —around 2,700 square feet (250 square meters)! If it were all laid out flat, it would be the size of a tennis court! This is because there are lots of folds all along it. These are lined with tiny finger-shaped hairs called villi. They absorb nutrients from food and pass them into blood in the **veins** running through your intestines. The blood goes up into your liver to be processed.

This is a magnified image of the villi in the small intestines. The food washes over them, and they extract the nutrients.

Millions of Villi

There are over 5 million villi lining the small intestines, each about 0.04 inch (1 millimeter) long. If you joined them end to end, they would stretch over 250 miles (400 kilometers)!

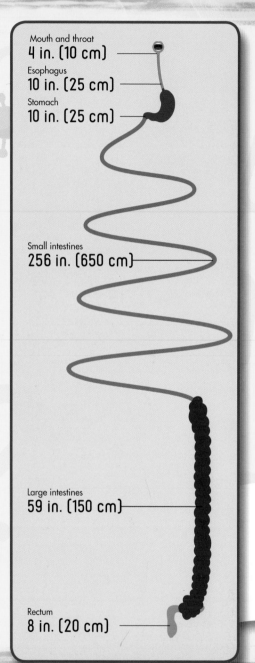

Mouth and throat
4 in. (10 cm)

Esophagus
10 in. (25 cm)

Stomach
10 in. (25 cm)

Small intestines
256 in. (650 cm)

Large intestines
59 in. (150 cm)

Rectum
8 in. (20 cm)

Large (but Short) Intestines

As the food reaches the end of your small intestines, not many nutrients are left in it. The food then passes into your large intestines. These are much shorter than your small intestines—only 5 feet (1.5 meters) long. But they are much wider—around 2 inches (5 centimeters) wide. This is why they are called the large intestines.

Your large intestines remove water and some of the remaining nutrients from the food. About 80 percent of the water is removed in your small intestines, and the large intestines remove some of the rest. Whatever is left over passes down to the bottom end of the large intestines to be disposed of later…

This diagram shows the lengths of parts of the digestive system. The small intestines are the longest part, followed by the large intestines.

Bacteria in the Bowels

About 500 types of bacteria live in your large intestines. These get to work on the undigested remains of your food. They break it down more, producing gas as they do so! They also make vitamin K, and they help your body to release important chemicals called **hormones**. In total, there are about 100 trillion bacteria in your large intestines!

Oops, Pardon!

Gas in the large intestines has to come out of the body, or else you would blow up like a balloon! When the gas leaves the body, out of the bottom, it is politely known as "passing gas." You may know of another word! Men "pass gas" around 14–25 times a day, while women do it around 7–12 times a day.

It is important to have bacteria in your intestines. Some people like to have drinks with extra bacteria added. These drinks claim to improve digestion.

Waste Products

After your food has passed through your large intestines, your body has no more use for it. Anything left over is stored at the end of your large intestines, to be got rid of later in the toilet.

Storage and Disposal

Feces (poops) are stored in the **rectum**, at the bottom end of the large intestines. When you are ready to go to the bathroom and get rid of them, you squeeze them through a hole called the anus, and into the toilet.

One normal, daily, single poop weighs about 4–9 ounces (100–250 grams). So, over a year, the average person produces about 79–200 pounds (36–91 kilograms) of feces. But that's nothing compared to an African elephant—it produces about 165 pounds (75 kilograms) of feces a day. That's 60,000 pounds (27,000 kilograms) a year!

You can usually smell when a baby needs its diaper changed!

Smelly!

Feces smell because of the bacteria in your intestines. It's the waste products that the bacteria make as they chomp on your undigested food that give poop its bad smell.

What's in Poop?

Feces are made of bits of food your body can't digest, such as fiber. They also contain bacteria and water. They are usually a brown color, because of the bile they contain.

This pie chart shows what is in a normal poop.

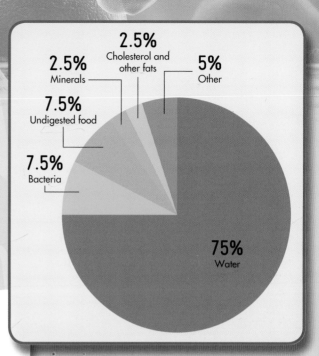

2.5%
Cholesterol and other fats

2.5%
Minerals

5%
Other

7.5%
Undigested food

7.5%
Bacteria

75%
Water

Fancy Coffee?

Black Ivory coffee is made in Thailand—from coffee beans in elephant poop! The elephants are fed on the coffee beans. As these pass through an elephant's digestive system, enzymes break down the bitter proteins in the coffee beans. They come out in the elephant's feces and are made into very smooth —and very expensive— coffee. It costs around $50 a cup!

What Poops Do You Do?

Sometimes, special doctors examine people's feces. Feces can tell us a lot about how well the body is working, what the diet of a person is like, and what might be wrong with someone who is sick. Feces can be classified into seven different types, depending on their size, shape, and hardness.

1	Tiny, hard little lumps like mini-eggs; hard to push out
2	Sausage shaped but very hard, like joined-up type 1 lumps; also hard to push out
3	Sausage shaped, smoother, slight cracks on surface; easier to push out
4	Very smooth, soft sausage; easy to push out
5	Soft and smooth, but come out in smaller lumps
6	Comes out quite suddenly, very soft and quite watery; floats in toilet
7	Comes out very suddenly; very watery with no solid lumps

This chart describes how some doctors classify feces. Types 3, 4, and 5 are normal for most people. Types 1 and 2 are staying inside the body a bit too long. Types 6 and 7 are not staying inside long enough!

If you need to do a type 7 poop, you might need to make a run for it!

Liquid Waste

Feces are (usually) solid wastes that come out the end of the digestive system. But the body also gets rid of liquid waste in the form of urine, or pee. Urine contains chemicals and extra water that the body doesn't need. It is made in two organs called **kidneys**. These clean the blood and remove the waste and extra water. Depending on how much you drink, you make about 3.2 pints (1.5 liters) of urine a day. That's over 1,057 pints (500 liters) a year—enough to fill almost five baths!

Asparagus, Anyone? Beets?

Asparagus contains chemicals high in sulfur. These chemicals can come out in your urine and make it smell a bit odd. But scientists think that only some people can detect the smell. Are you one of the lucky ones? Beets contains colored chemicals that can make urine look pink or red.

Cleaning in the Kidneys

Blood passes through your kidneys all the time. Every day, your kidneys clean about 475 gallons (1,800 liters) of blood! An average adult has 10–12 pints (5–6 liters) of blood in his or her body, so each drop of blood passes through the kidneys over 300 times in a day.

The kidneys remove waste products carried by the blood from other parts of your body. The blood also carries a waste product called urea. This is made in your liver as it breaks down proteins from food. In your kidneys, the waste products (including urea) mix with water to make urine.

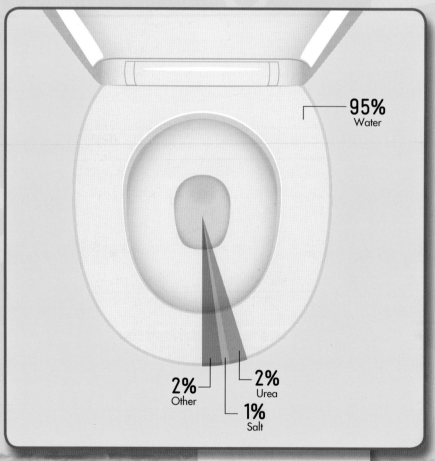

95%
Water

2%
Other

2%
Urea

1%
Salt

This diagram shows what normal urine is made of.

Color-Testing

Urine is usually a clear yellowish color. Different foods can change the color. The color is also affected by how much water you drink. Sometimes a strange color can indicate a health problem. Cloudy urine can also mean that there is some kind of infection or disease in the body.

Pale yellow	Perfectly normal
Dark yellow, orange	Need to drink a bit more water; have been drinking colored drinks or eating carrots
Brown	Have been eating fava beans, aloe, or rhubarb; may have a liver problem
Red	Have been eating blueberries, colored drinks, or beets; if it looks like blood, see a doctor
Blue, dark green	Have been eating asparagus; if not, see a doctor
Oily	Have been eating lots of fried food

Feeling Thirsty?

A man who dislocated his hip while walking in the Spanish mountains had to wait six days before being found and rescued. He survived by drinking sips of…his own urine.

Where Does the Pee Go?

After it is made in the kidneys, urine trickles down tubes called ureters. These are about 12 inches (30 centimeters) long, and they take the urine down to the bladder. This is a pear-shaped, stretchy bag that stores your urine. When it is empty, it is about the size of your thumb. It stretches as more and more urine fills it, and eventually starts to send signals to your brain, telling you to empty it!

This diagram shows how your bladder stretches as it fills up with urine. The more it stretches, the more you feel the need to empty it.

Thumb sized
No urge
to urinate

0.6 pint (300 ml)
Slight urge
to urinate

1 pint (500 ml)
Strong urge
to urinate

1.3 pints (600 ml)
Desperate urge
to urinate

Big Bladder

Every time an elephant pees, it gets rid of 6–12 pints (5–10 liters). Imagine the size of its bladder! A large whale's bladder can hold 31–42 pints (15–20 liters) of urine. In contrast, a rat's bladder only holds about 0.04 ounce (1 milliliter) of urine.

Aaaaah, That's Better

When you go to the bathroom, a little muscle at the bottom end of your bladder relaxes. Your urine comes down and out through a tube called the urethra, and into the toilet. Your bladder empties like a deflating balloon, and the urge to pee disappears.

The urethra in a woman is about 1.6 inches (4 centimeters) long. In a man, the urethra is about 7.9 inches (20 centimeters) long… You can guess why the male one is longer!

This diagram shows the parts of your body that deal with getting rid of urine.

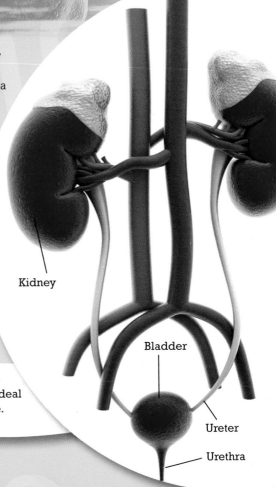

Kidney

Bladder

Ureter

Urethra

Cooling Down and Cleaning Up

Some vultures pee on their legs when they get hot. As the urine evaporates, it cools them down. The strong acid in the urine also helps to get rid of any germs that may have gotten onto their legs from the rotting meat that they eat.

Digestive Problems

Just like all the body systems, the digestive system can have its problems.

Acid Stomachs

The stomach is coated with a layer of thick, slimy mucus to protect it from the acids in the gastric juices. Sometimes the mucus coating can be damaged (for example, by bad bacteria in the stomach or by certain painkilling drugs that people swallow). The acid can then attack the wall of the stomach, causing painful sores called **ulcers**.

The acidity of something can be measured using a **pH scale**. The most acidic things have a pH of 0. Water is neutral, with a pH of 7. A pH higher than 7 means the substance is not acidic, but is increasingly **alkaline**. Stomach acid has a pH level of 2.

Battery acid	pH0
Stomach acid	pH2
Lemon juice/vinegar	pH2
Grapefruit	pH3
Tomato juice	pH4
Black coffee	pH5
Urine	pH5–pH8
Water	pH7
Sea water	pH8
Baking soda	pH9
Soap	pH12
Bleach	pH13
Drain cleaner	pH14

Poop Type 7+

Sometimes people have **diarrhea**. This is when their feces are very watery. Diarrhea can be caused by lots of things, including a virus such as norovirus. It can be caused by bacteria in rotten food, or tiny **parasites** such as giardia in dirty water. When you have diarrhea, food passes extremely quickly through your digestive system. Your body absorbs hardly anything from it, including water, and so you produce very watery feces.

Washing your hands thoroughly after using the bathroom, and before handling or eating food, is the best way to avoid catching and spreading stomach bugs.

Winter Vomiting Bug

Norovirus is also known as the winter vomiting bug, because it is more common in winter and causes vomiting as well as diarrhea. It causes about 20 million cases of diarrhea in the United States every year.

You Are What You Eat

Everything you eat is processed by your digestive system. The food is either used by your body or comes out as feces. Some people eat too much and get too little exercise. Some eat too many foods that are high in fat or have lots of carbohydrates. This can lead to people gaining weight, because the body stores extra energy from food as fat. Some people become **obese**—very overweight. This can cause lots of health problems, including heart conditions, diabetes, and joint problems.

Global Obesity

The World Heath Organization estimates that at least 2.8 million people around the world die every year as a result of being overweight or obese.

Percentage of obese people
- Less than 10
- 10–19.9
- 20–29.9
- Over 30
- No figures available

This map shows the percentage of obese people in countries around the world. Use the colors in the key to figure out which countries have the most obese people.

Feeding the World

More and more people in developed countries such as the United States and United Kingdom are becoming obese. At the same time, over 900 million people in the world are suffering from malnutrition because they do not have enough food to eat.

This is not because the world doesn't produce enough food to feed everyone. In fact, global food production produces 17 percent more calories per person than it did 30 years ago, even though the world population has increased by 70 percent in that time! The main problem is that millions of people don't have enough money to buy food.

Not having enough food does not just make you thin, it means you are less able to fight diseases and infection. It also means you will be lacking in energy and can make you dizzy and depressed. In the end, it can kill you. Around 2.6 million child deaths every year are linked to malnutrition.

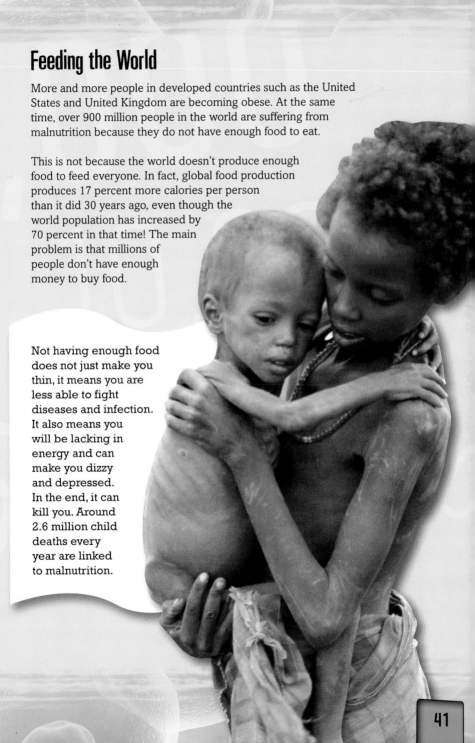

You're in Control!

Your digestive system is your food factory. It turns yummy food into all the energy, vitamins, minerals, proteins, and other chemicals that your body needs. You decide what goes through your digestive system every time you eat. So make sure you make good food choices, because you can't control what happens after you've eaten it!

All in the Mind

Your digestive system does not work separately from your other body systems. Your blood flow connects to your digestive system so that the blood can carry the chemicals from the food all around your body. Your kidneys and bladder work with your digestive system to remove waste from your body.

Your body systems are all linked and need to work together. They are all controlled by your brain. Messages sent to and from your digestive system and other body parts travel along nerve cells. These messages can travel at up to 270 miles (435 kilometers) per hour. They travel around the nervous system—a network of 93,000 miles (150,000 kilometers) of nerves in your body.

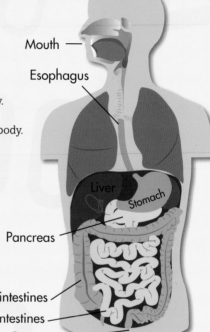

Mouth

Esophagus

Liver

Stomach

Pancreas

Large intestines

Small intestines

Rectum

Hormones

Hormones are chemicals that are made in special glands in your body, and also in your stomach, intestines, and kidneys. They help to control your digestive system. For example, the hormone gastrin triggers your body to make stomach juices.

Watery Bodies

Your body is about two-thirds water. Water makes up 80 percent of your blood, 75 percent of your brain, and 20 percent of your bones. Most people need to take in about 4 pints (2 liters) of water every day, through their food and drink. Lots of chemicals in your body are transported by water. Water also helps you to chew, swallow, and wash down food.

Your 30-foot (9-meter) digestive system gives you the fuel you need to live, grow, repair, move, and think. Make sure you take care of it—and it will take care of you.

Test Yourself!

Take a look at the questions below. You will find all the answers somewhere in this book. Check out the pages where the information is if you need reminding of the answers.

1 How wide is the tube that makes up the large intestines?
a   2 inches (5 centimeters)
b   4 inches (10 centimeters)
c   0.4 inch (1 centimeter)

2 How much liquid does a person drink in an average lifetime?
a   2,600 gallons (10,000 liters)
b   20,000 gallons (75,000 liters)
c   40,000 gallons (150,000 liters)

3 Which portion of food would give you the energy to run the farthest?
a   a package of peanuts
b   a portion of chicken
c   a slice of bread

4 How much saliva does an average person produce every day?
a   none
b   about 1 pint (500 milliliters)
c   more than 2 pints (1 liter)

5 What are feces mostly made of?
a   fat
b   undigested food
c   water

6 Put these parts of the digestive system in order, starting from the first part that your food meets.
small intestines; mouth; stomach; rectum; esophagus; throat; large intestines

7 Most people get most of their vitamin D from:

a their food
b sunlight
c water

8 If a chocolate bar contains 250 kilocalories of energy, which is equal to 1,050 kilojoules of energy, how many kilojoules are in 1 kilocalorie?

a 2
b 4
c 4.2

9 Which organ does over 500 different jobs, creates warmth in your body, and is your second-biggest organ?

a heart
b stomach
c liver

10 Which of these is more acidic than the juices in your stomach?

a battery acid
b water
c lemon juice

Mystery Organ

There is a strange little organ attached to your large intestines, just where it joins the small intestines. It is a worm-like muscular pouch, about 3½ inches (9 centimeters) long. No one really knows what it is for! Scientists think that long ago, when early humans ate tough things like tree bark, this mystery organ helped to break them down. Do some research to try to find out the name of this organ.

Answers:
1a; 2b; 3a; 4c; 5c; 6: mouth, throat, esophagus, stomach, small intestines, large intestines, rectum; 7b; 8: 1 kcal = 4.2 kJ; 9c; 10a

Glossary

abdomen part of the body between the chest and the hips

alkaline liquid that has a pH level higher than 7

bacteria tiny living things that you can't see, but that live on and in your body. Some types of bacteria are harmless, while others can cause illnesses and disease.

clot form sticky lumps of blood cells

diabetic person who has diabetes

diarrhea illness that causes someone's feces to be very watery and very frequent

enzyme protein that helps a chemical reaction take place inside a living thing

gland body part that produces chemicals that are either released into the body or pass out of the body

glucagon chemical produced by the pancreas that increases the level of glucose in the blood

hormone chemical made in the body; hormones move around in the blood and affect certain organs

insulin chemical produced by the pancreas that lowers the level of glucose in the blood

intestine long, coiled tube, below the stomach

kidney one of two organs in the body that remove water and waste from the blood and send them to the bladder as urine

mineral substance formed in the Earth's crust

mucus slimy, sticky material that the body produces to protect certain parts of it

nerve cell tiny building block. Nerve cells link all parts of your body to your brain.

obese very overweight and with a lot of body fat

organ part of your body that performs a particular task; for example, your heart is an organ that pumps blood around your body

parasite plant, animal, or other living thing that lives on or inside another living thing

pH scale way of telling how alkaline or acidic a liquid is, by measuring the power of the hydrogen particles in it

protein substance that is made up of nitrogen, carbon, oxygen, hydrogen, and other chemicals

pulse seed found in the pods of plants such as peas or lentils

rectum bottom end of the large intestines where feces (poops) are stored

reflex response or reaction of the body that is not chosen or controlled by conscious thought

tissue group of cells (tiny building blocks) that are like each other and do similar things

ulcer open sore on or in the body

vein blood vessel that carries blood from around the body toward the heart

Find Out More

BOOKS

Burstein, John. *The Dynamic Digestive System: How Does My Stomach Work?* (Slim Goodbody's Body Buddies). Ontario, Canada: Crabtree, 2009.

Dudley Gold, Susan. *Learning about the Digestive and Excretory Systems* (Learning about the Human Body Systems). Berkeley Heights, N.J.: Enslow, 2013.

Prior, Jennifer. *The Digestive System* (TIME for Kids Nonfiction Readers). Huntington Beach, Calif.: Teacher Created Materials, 2011.

Sohn, Emily. *A Journey Through the Digestive System with Max Axiom, Super Scientist* (Graphic Science). Mankato, Minn.: Capstone, 2009.

Taylor-Butler, Christine. *The Digestive System* (True Books). New York: Scholastic, 2008.

WEB SITES

kids.discovery.com/tell-me/science/body-systems/your-digestive-system

This web site from Discovery Kids is full of information and fascinating facts about the journey your food takes through your body.

kidshealth.org/kid/htbw/digestive_system.html

Here you can find out lots of information about the digestive system, and there are diagrams to click on and find out more.

www.realcooljobs.com/come-and-visit/whats-on/freaky-nature/top-poo-facts.php

On this fun web site, you can roll down the roll of toilet paper to find out lots of interesting facts about poop!

FURTHER RESEARCH

You could visit your local library to see if there are any books on the digestive system. You could also make some observations about your own digestive system! Keep a food diary of all the things you eat and drink. See if you can find out about the nutritional value of your food—how much energy it gives you, which vitamins and minerals it contains, and how much fat and sugar it contains.

Index